NATIONAL GEOGRAPHIC

T0308469

MAKING FACES

PIONEER EDITION

By Ronald Naversen and Lori Wilkinson

CONTENTS

Making

Faces

By Ronald Naversen

Professor of Theater, Southern Illinois University Carbondale

My young neighbor was shocked. It was her first visit to my house. Everywhere she turned, faces stared back. There were big faces. There were small faces. Some were bright. Others were plain. She said, "You really have an interesting place here!"

My house is filled with masks. I have about 150. Masks amaze me. They are powerful. They change how people look and act!

I take trips to study masks. In Greece, I watched people make masks. They were just like the masks used long ago. Actors wore masks in plays back then.

I went to Romania, too. The trip was great. There I saw masks change people into hairy, wild men. Then I went to New Orleans and New York. I watched people parade in masks.

Colorful Character.
A masked dancer performs at a festival in Bhutan.

4

Full of Spirit

One of my favorite trips was to Bali. It is an island in Indonesia. I learned to carve wooden masks there.

Carving masks is hard. After artists carve the masks, they paint them. They use many colors. Some mask makers add hair or jewels.

The masks are used in plays. The plays are about good and evil. People in Bali believe a mask has a spirit. They think a mask holds the **character** it shows. The masks help actors act like those characters.

Festival Faces

People in Bhutan use masks the same way. Bhutan is a small nation in Asia. Their masks show spirits, demons, and other characters.

Dancers wear masks at **festivals**. The dances tell tales from their religion, known as Buddhism.

The audience knows each character by its mask. That helps people follow the stories. These stories tell how to lead a good life.

5

Facing Change

The Dogon people live in West Africa. Each village has its own kind of mask. Some masks are tall. Some are taller than a man. Others look like cloth bags covered with shells. Some have tall, thin wood pieces on top. Some are simple wooden faces.

Dancers perform in masks when someone dies. They dance on the roof of the person's house. That shows respect for the dead person.

The Dogon also wear masks to dance at festivals. This helps keep Dogon traditions alive. That's important to the Dogon. The world is changing. And they don't want their **culture** to die out.

Wearing the Wolf

Masks are not the only way to make faces. Some people put paint or ink on their faces.

The Northern Arapaho people live in Wyoming. They wear face paint. They also wear headdresses. They want to look like wolves. The wolf is special to them.

The Northern Arapaho believe wolves are teachers. Long ago, people watched wolves. Then the people learned to hunt. They also learned how to share food. Now the Northern Arapaho honor wolves with dances. Dancers use face paint to look the part.

Wolf Dance. *A Northern Arapaho man is ready for a gathering. He wears a wolf headdress and face paint.*

Warrior Welcome. *Group members in Papua New Guinea use masks to honor young warriors.*

Read My Face

The Maori people are from New Zealand. Their faces tell stories with **designs**. One side of a man's face tells about his dad. The other side tells about his mom.

The face designs are permanent. This means they will not wash off. Artists cut the design into the skin. Then they put color into the cuts. That makes blue-black marks.

Getting face designs hurts. But the Maori think the pain is okay. That's because the designs show they are part of the group.

Standing Out

The Karo are a people in Ethiopia. That is in East Africa. They live near a larger group. Both groups are alike.

The Karo could be lost in the larger group. But they want to stand out. So they paint their faces. Their face paint says, "Look at me. I am proud to be Karo!"

Familiar Faces

I travel far and wide to see masks. Yet I can see masks in my own life, too. Kids wear masks with costumes. Sports fans paint their faces in the colors of their team.

All over the world, a new face is a chance to act like a new person. That is why making faces has such power.

Wordwise

character: a person in a story or play

culture: a group's beliefs, language, arts, and way of life

design: pattern or shape, usually considered pleasing

festival: celebration that sometimes lasts for days

Big Day. *Young Aborigine boys in Australia get ready for a gathering. There they will learn the ways of their people.*

One of a Kind. *Face paint helps the Karo people stand out from other groups.*

Shadows and Light

By Lori Wilkinson

THEY HAVE A SPECIAL WAY to tell stories in Java. They tell stories with shadow puppets.

Wayang Puppet Theater is an old tradition. People have been telling stories this way for 1,000 years.

People in Indonesia still use puppets to tell their stories today.

Performance Traditions. Performers hang up a sheet. They stay behind it. They shine a light against the sheet. Then, a *dalang,* or puppeteer, holds up the puppets. The light shines on them. This makes shadows on the sheet.

There are also singers and musicians behind the sheet. They play music. The music helps the stories come to life.

Story Traditions. The *dalang* tells the stories. Some are about history. Some are about myths and legends. And some are about religion or heroes.

Dalangs start to learn these stories as children. One famous *dalang* started performing when he was only twelve years old!

Puppet Traditions. Puppets can be made of wood or leather. Some are rounded. Some are flat. They all have canes attached. These are long sticks. The sticks make the puppets' arms and legs move.

The Wayang Kulit is a kind of puppet. It is flat. It's made from buffalo leather.

Traditions in the Future. Will people watch shadow puppets in the future? UNESCO (United Nations Educational, Scientific, and Cultural Organization) believes Wayang Puppet Theater is important. It should be "safeguarded." This means people will try hard to keep the tradition safe. If Wayang Puppet Theater is safe, then many people will watch the shows for many more years.

Center Stage

Try on what you have learned about performers. Then answer these questions.

1 Why are masks powerful?

2 Look at the photos on pages 5 and 6. How are the two dancers different?

3 What is the article "Making Faces" mostly about?

4 How do people in Java use shadow puppets to tell stories?

5 How do people use masks and puppets to preserve traditions?